Knight Boo
Christmas Fun

All the fun of Christmas: the stories and traditions of the
festive days; how to make decorations, cards and presents.
Games and tricks, too, special recipes and party plans. And
if you want to do a nativity play or pantomime with your
friends there are helpful hints and scripts.

Merry Christmas..

Knight Book of
CHRISTMAS FUN

Gyles Brandreth

Illustrated by Barry Raynor

 KNIGHT BOOKS

the paperback division of Brockhampton Press

ISBN 0 340 19021 3

First published 1974 by Knight the paperback division of Brockhampton Press, Leicester.

Text copyright ⓒ 1974 Gyles Brandreth
Illustrations copyright ⓒ 1974 Brockhampton Press

Printed and bound in Great Britain by Cox and Wyman Ltd., London, Reading and Fakenham.

Contents

CHRISTMAS CALENDAR

Christmas Calendar

No one knows if Jesus was really born on 25th December, but mid-winter has always been a time for festivity and merry-making, and to Christians 25th December seems as good a day as any for celebrating the birthday of Jesus. He was born in Bethlehem, a village near the ancient city of Jerusalem, in the country that is now called Israel, almost two thousand years ago, and it is after Jesus that the Christmas we know is named.

But long before Jesus was born, people chose this time of year as a time of celebration. The Ancient Romans always had a lot of fun in December. Their wild festival of sun and light, the Saturnalia, began on 17th December and lasted a whole week, quickly followed up by their New Year celebrations. In between, on 25th December, they marked the Birthday of the Unconquered Sun in a grand style. If anything, the celebrations of the Ancient Romans were even livelier than ours are today. During the Saturnalia, people ran riot, masters and servants changed clothes and the entertainment went on non-stop. And at New Year, not only did everyone eat, drink and make merry for three whole days, they also gave each other presents.

The Romans weren't the only ones to have a bit of a party in the middle of December. In Northern Europe there was the special Yule Festival, marking the turn of the year on 21st December. People filled their homes with bright lights, evergreens and fires, and exchanged gifts and good wishes for the coming months.

The Romans, the Norsemen, the Celts and the Teutons all had important mid-winter celebrations, so that the Christians - some of whom in the early days had celebrated the birthday of Jesus on 1st January or 29th March or 29th September - were fitting in with a long tradition when they finally chose 25th December as Christmas day.

The Feast of Saint Nicholas

To Christians, 6th December, the Feast day of Saint Nicholas, is the beginning of the Christmas season. The <u>real</u> Saint Nicholas, the patron Saint of Russia, Aberdeen, sailors, scholars, merchants, pawnbrokers and small boys, was the Bishop of Myra 1,500 years ago and performed several miracles, including one where he brought three boys back to life after they had been pickled in a tub of brine!

There is another, rather more exciting Saint Nicholas, of course, and he is the one who visits the homes of children on 6th December. He travels on horseback and if you want him to leave you a present, you must leave a carrot and some water outside your door for his horse. Some people say he also travels with a fierce character called Black Peter, who beats all the bad children while Saint Nicholas is giving presents to all the good ones. Saint Nicholas only brings small gifts = pieces of fruit, sweets and cakes - and nowadays only seems to have a large following in places like Germany, Austria, Holland and the Scandinavian countries.

This Saint Nicholas is probably related to our own Father Christmas, who travels with his reindeer, and turns up on Christmas Eve. In fact, Santa Claus, the other name for Father Christmas, comes from 'Sinte Klaas' which is how some of the Dutch settlers in America used to pronounce the name of Saint Nicholas.

Whether or not you believe in Saint Nicholas, whether or not you leave out a carrot and some water for his horse, 6th December is the day to begin putting up all your Christmas decorations.

Christmas Eve

By 24th December, Christmas Eve, all your decorations should be up, all your cards posted, all your presents chosen and wrapped. Many Christians - mostly grown-ups - go to a special church service on Christmas Eve called midnight Mass. Any many others - mostly children - spend Christmas Eve wondering what Father Christmas is going to bring them.

One old Christmas Eve tradition that has sadly disappeared is the custom of dragging in the Yule log. In fuedal days when all the large households had enormous fires, people would go out into the woods on Christmas Eve, find a large log, decorate it with colourful ribbons and drag it home to burn. If you passed anyone dragging home a Yule log you had to lift your hat and greet them, because the Yule log was supposed to bring good luck, and the burning of it marked the end of old quarrels.

The old Yule log was lit on Christmas Eve and burned through the Twelve Days of Christmas, from 25th December until 6th January. The ashes were then stored until the next year and were meant to protect the house from fire and lightning. No one who squinted was allowed into the room where the Yule log was burning and no woman with bare feet or flat feet was allowed in either!.

Today almost no one has a proper Yule log, but a lot of people do have a token Yule log, made of chocolate cake. It isn't as lucky as the real thing, but if you make a wish when you cut it your wish is supposed to come true.

Christmas Day

Christmas Day, 25th December, is the day when Christians go to church to celebrate the birth of Jesus and when Father Christmas pays his annual call. Father Christmas travels the world in a flying sleigh drawn by reindeer. At least, that's what people think. A hundred years ago, everybody believed his sleigh was drawn by horses, but the Americans introduced the idea of the reindeer and it could well be true. Nobody knows for sure, of course, because nobody has ever met Father Christmas face to face.

Christmas Day is a day for going to church, for opening the presents from Father Christmas and for exchanging gifts among the family. It is also the day for Christmas Dinner. Some people have it at lunchtime, some people have it at suppertime, but most people enjoy it whenever they have it. Roast turkey and mince pies and Christmas pudding are among the traditional things we eat on 25th December. If we're very lucky, we get a slice of Christmas cake as well. Some people put small charms - rings and bells and lucky horseshoes - in their Christmas cake and others put in silver coins which will bring luck to whoever finds one in their piece of cake. Luck certainly comes to anyone who stirs the cake mixture and makes a wish before the cake is baked.

Boxing Day

Boxing Day has got nothing to do with people punching each other on the nose. No one is completely sure how it got the name, but it is probably something to do with the fact that the alms-boxes in churches, where people left money for the church or for the poor, were opened on the day after Christmas, and the fact that apprentices used to tour the homes of their employers with pottery boxes on 26th December hoping for a gift of money.

26th December is also the Feast day of Saint Stephen, the very first Christian to be killed and martyred for his beliefs, and for no very good reason he is a Saint particularly associated with horses - which may be one of the reasons why Boxing Day is a traditional day for huntsmen to meet on horseback with their fox-hounds and go for a hunt. It is also the day on which the pantomime season traditionally starts and many people go to see a pantomime or Christmas play on the afternoon or evening of Boxing Day.

New Year's Eve

31st December, the last day of one year and the eve of the next, is a day when a lot of people give a party to 'see the old year out and welcome the new year in'. At the stroke of midnight everyone must wish everyone else a 'Happy New Year' and, putting on their best Scots accent, sing the words of the famous Scottish poet, Robert Burns:

> *Should auld acquaintance be forgot,*
> *And never brought to mind?*
> *Should auld acquaintance be forgot,*
> *And auld lang syne?*

> *For auld lang syne, my dear,*
> *For auld lang syne,*
> *We'll tak' a cup o' kindness yet*
> *For auld lang syne.*

New Year's Day

In Scotland 1st January is a special day and the New Year celebrations are taken very seriously. 'First Footing' is the most important of their New Year traditions and the First Footer - the first person to set a foot through your door on New Year's day - can bring you lots of luck. Of course, not any old First Footer will do: according the custom, the luckiest First Footer will be a dark-haired man who is a stranger (but doesn't squint and isn't flat-footed) who arrives on the door-step carrying a piece of coal, a pinch of salt, a loaf of bread and some money!

New Year's Day is also the day when people all over the world make their New Year resolutions. They decide that in the New Year they are not going to be lazy or greedy or naughty, that they are not going to tell lies and that they are going to give up sweets and clean their teeth twice a day. If they are very lucky (and very good), their New Year resolutions will last till Twelfth Night.

Twelfth Night

6th January is the Feast of the Epiphany, the day for Christians that marks the visit of the three Wise Men to the baby Jesus in Bethlehem. They brought with them gifts of gold, frankincense and myrrh and the occasion is still marked with special church services. One of them takes place at the Chapel Royal in St. James's Palace in London, where two Gentlemen Ushers make offerings of gold, frankincense and myrrh, on behalf of the Queen. The gold is represented by twenty-five gold sovereigns and is later given to old poor people, the frankincense (which is a perfumed incense) goes to a church and the myrrh (which can be used in medicine) is given to a hospital.

6th January also marks the twelfth day of Christmas and the end of the Christmas season. It is on Twelfth Night that all the Christmas decorations and cards have to be taken down and put away. If you leave your decorations up after Twelfth Night, the most dreadful things are supposed to happen to you. Robert Herrick, the seventeenth century English poet, wrote a verse about it:

Down with the rosemary and so,
Down with the baies and mistletoe,
Down with the holly, ivy, all,
Wherewith ye dressed the Christmas hall.

That so the superstitious find
Not one least branch there left behind,
For look, how many leaves there be
Neglected there, maids trust to me,
So many goblins you shall see.

CHRISTMAS DECORATIONS

Christmas Decorations

One of the traditions of Christmas is that you decorate your home - with a Christmas tree, with holly and ivy, with mistletoe and all sorts of artificial decorations, like balloons and paper chains and Christmas crackers. If you have a garden or live in the country, you may be able to pick your own holly and ivy and mistletoe, but if you don't have a garden or live in a town, you will have to buy it from your local greengrocer.

You can buy all sorts of artificial decorations too - baubles for the tree, paper chains for the walls, cardboard cut-outs to stick on the window - but it's more fun (and less expensive) to make your own and most of the ideas in this chapter are for do-it-yourself Christmas decorations that don't take long to make but give a lot of pleasure. Some of the decorations you will hang on your tree, some you will hang from the lightshade, some you will stick on the windows, some you will stick on the walls, some you will lay out on top of a spare table or chest of drawers, some you will move about - all of them will brighten your home between 6th December and 6th January.

Christmas Trees

The tradition of Christmas trees has been around for a very long time. Way back in 1605 a German merchant from Strasbourg recorded: 'At Christmas they set up fir trees in the parlour at Strasbourg and hang on them roses cut out of many-coloured paper, apples, biscuits, gold-foil and sweets' - so the idea of the gaily decorated Christmas tree has obviously been popular in some parts of the world for almost four hundred years.

It didn't reach Great Britain until about one hundred and fifty years ago and it only became really popular over here when Queen Victoria's husband, Prince Albert, set the fashion and made everyone feel that no Christmas party could be complete without a Christmas tree. Nowadays, of course, almost everybody has one - big ones, small ones, real ones, toy ones - and if you want to see a truly enormous one you must visit Trafalgar Square in London at Christmastime where you can see the giant Christmas tree that the people of Oslo have given to the people of London every year since 1946.

Even if your Christmas tree isn't as big as the one in Trafalgar Square, you can still have a lot of fun decorating it. If you want to hang lights on the tree, you will have to buy them because candles on a tree aren't really safe. You can put all sorts of other things on your Christmas tree: decorations brought from a shop, home-made decorations like some of the ones described later on in this chapter, tangerines, sweets, Christmas crackers, Christmas presents, anything you like in fact - so long as the decorations aren't too heavy and don't make the tree topple over!

Holly and Ivy

HOLLY

Holly, with its shining green leaves and bright red berries, makes a very pretty Christmas decoration. You can do all sorts of things with holly branches and with individual leaves. You can put branches over pictures, over doorways, over curtain-rails, on top of the bookshelves, on top of mantel-pieces and make a room look very festive. You can take one or two holly leaves and with a little sticky tape stick them into the door of your room or onto your windows.

The more you use holly at Christmas the luckier you will be, because people say that holly brings good luck. The Red Indians of North America even say that holly can cure the measles!

IVY

Holly and Ivy go together at Christmas and all the things you can do with holly you can do with ivy as well. Ivy brings you luck too and if you're frightened of witches it's just the thing you need. According to an old superstition, wicked witches are terrified of ivy and won't come anywhere near it.

If you are someone who likes to sing while you work, here is the beginning of a very famous Christmas carol for you to sing while you are decorating you home with holly and ivy:

> The holly and the ivy,
>   When they are both full grown,
> Of all the tress that are in the wood,
>   The holly bears the crown.

> O the rising of the sun,
>   And the running of the deer,
> The playing of the merry organ,
>   Sweet singing in the choir.

Balloons and Mistletoe

BALLOONS

Balloons make marvellous Christmas decorations, but don't put them all up on 6th December because, if you do, you will find that half of them will have burst or shrivelled away by Christmas Day! Put up a few at a time, and when you've blown them tie a knot round them with string, so that it air does escape and they do shrink, you can always untie the knot and blow them up all over again.

MISTLETOE

In days of old mistletoe was one of the most magical of all plants. If you had a bit of mistletoe in your home you would be protected from thunder, lightning, evil spells and black magic. And if you kept some mistletoe in your medicine chest, it would cure you of all sorts of terrible diseases.

Today nobody seems to believe in the magic power of mistletoe, but at Christmas it still serves a purpose. People hang it up in their homes and kiss underneath it. You can hang it most easily from a light-shade and then whenever anybody you would like to kiss happens to be standing underneath it, you can go over and claim a kiss and they are not allowed to refuse you.

Christmas Cards

Christmas cards make attractive decorations. You can stand
them up on tables and desks and mantel-pieces and, better
still, you can pin them to curtains. If you get a lot, you can
pin them to long pieces of ribbon or long strips of coloured
paper and stick the ribbon or the paper onto a wall with
sticky tape. If you and your parents are clever, you may
have kept last year's Christmas cards, which means that you
can decorate your room with cards - pinning them to the
curtains, pinning them to strips of coloured crepe paper,
sticking them onto the windows with sticky tape - right at
the beginning of December, long before the postman has
brought you any new cards of your own.

Christmas Crackers

To make crackers all you need are some old toilet rolls, coloured crepe paper and coloured string. Take the empty toilet roll, roll it up in a piece of crepe paper that is roughly two inches longer than the toilet roll at each end and tie up both ends with string:

What you must remember to do, of course, is <u>fill</u> the crackers you make. You can put some sweets inside or a small toy or a balloon or a nut, and you must always include a riddle. You can write the riddle on a small slip of paper, putting the question on one side and the answer on the other. Here are a few to get you going:

Q: When the clock strikes thirteen, what time is it?
A: Time to have the clock mended!

Q: I have a head and a tail, but no body. What am I?
A: A coin!

Q: Why is it always a mistake to put on a shoe?
A: Because you're always putting your foot in it!

Q: What has two heads, six feet, one tail and four ears?
A: A man on horseback!

Q: What gets wetter the more it dries?
A: A towel!

Q: What is worse than a giraffe with a sore throat?
A: A centipede with sore feet!

Q: Why are cooks cruel?
A: Because they beat eggs and whip cream!

Q: What often falls, but never gets hurt?
A: Rain!

Q: Mrs. Bigger had a baby. Who was bigger?
A: The baby, because he was a little Bigger!

Q: What question can never be answered honestly with the word 'Yes'?
A: 'Are you asleep?'!

Q: Why did the man stand behind the donkey?
A: Because he got a kick out of it!

Q: Where are the Kings and Queens of England usually crowned?
A: On the head!

Q: What starts with T, ends with T and is full of T?
A: A teapot!

Q: Who always goes to sleep with his shoes on?
A: A horse!

Q: Why did Noddy's mother knit him three socks?
A: Because he wrote to tell her that he'd grown another foot!

Q: What can speak in every language, but never went to school?
A: An echo!

Christmas Log

To make a Christmas Log, you will need a small log - about twelve or fifteen inches log - split in half, white paint, artifical snow, plasticine, candles, holly, fir cones and acorns. Begin by painting the log with white paint: don't cover it completely with the paint, but try to make it look as if the log has been lying out in the snow. While the paint is still wet, sprinkle some artificial snow over it.

Once the paint has dried, roll the plasticine into a long worm and place it along the top of the log. Now stick the decorations - the candles, the holly, the fir cones, the acorns - into the plasticine and sprinkle on some more artificial snow.

Christmas Mobile

To make a Christmas mobile you need a metal coat hanger, some stiff paper, coloured pencils, wool, cotton wool, glue, sticky tape, needle and thread, and a pair of scissors.

Begin by cutting out the shapes of faces or stars or Christmas trees. Four will do, and you can make them all the same or all different. If you want to make a Father Christmas face, start by drawing a circle onto your paper (you can use the roll of sticky tape to give you the shape of the circle), cut out the circle and draw on Father Christmas's eyes, nose, mouth and ears. Now stick on some hair and a beard using the cotton wool and glue.

If you want to make a cat, cut out the same circle and draw on the cat's ears, eyes, nose and mouth and then stick on some whiskers made of wool. If you want to make a star or a Christmas tree, just draw the right shape on the paper, cut it out and colour it.

When you have cut out and decorated your face shapes, thread the needle with the cotton and tie a large knot at the end. Now push the needle through the top of the first shape and pull the thread through. Do the same with the other three shapes, making sure that the length of thread you use is different each time.

Now tie the four threads with the shapes hanging from them onto a metal coat hanger. Bend the coat hanger a bit first to make a more interesting shape. Now hang the coat hanger from a lampshade in the middle of the room. It will look something like this:

25

Christmas Pompom

To make a Christmas pompom you will need two sheets of tissue paper in different colours, scissors and needle and thread. Begin by cutting out ten circles of tissue paper, five of them in one colour, five in another. To make sure your circle is completely round, you can trace the shape onto the tissue paper before you start cutting it, using the bottom of a mug or a milk bottle or even of a saucer to get the right shape.

Fold each circle of tissue paper in half, then in quarters. Then thread the needle and tie a large knot in the end. Now thread each folded circle through its corner onto the cotton, like this:

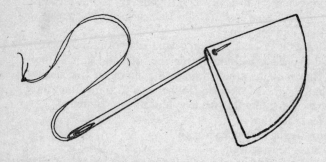

Thread one colour on, then the next, until all ten circles have been threaded onto the cotton when you must tie a firm knot in the end of the cotton. Now all you have to do is pull open each of the folded circles and you will find you have got a very pretty pompom that you can hang on the Christmas tree.

Father Christmasses all in a row

To make a row of Father Christmasses, you will need a long sheet of white paper, a pair of scissors and some coloured pencils. Begin by folding the paper, making the first fold about two inches from the top and folding it forward, making the next fold about two inches from the first and folding it backward, and so on. When you've finished, the folds will look something like this:

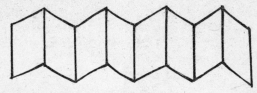

Now draw a picture of Father Christmas on the top fold, like this:

Now cut around the figure of Father Christmas, except where his clothes touch the edge of the paper. Open out the piece of paper and you'll find you have got a row of Father Christmasses ready for you to colour with your pencils.

Yoghurt Christmas Tree

No, this isn't a tree made of yoghurt: it's a tree made of <u>empty yoghurt cartons.</u> Collect ten of them and paint them all sorts of bright colours. If you like, paint faces on them, but whatever you do make them look as bright as possible.

When you've painted all the cartons and the paint has dried, pile the cartons up into a pyramid, like this:

If you like, cut out a star, stick it onto a thin piece of stick and poke it through the top carton.

Paper Chains

To make the easiest kind of Christmas paper chain all you
need to do is cut out short strips of coloured paper about
an inch wide and make them into interlocking loops. You
begin by making the first loop simply by sticking the two
ends of one strip of paper together. You thread the next
strip of paper through the first loop and then stick its ends
together. You do the same with the third strip and so it goes
on until you have got the right length of chain.

If you want to try something a bit more difficult, you
will need long strips of paper (crepe paper is very good) about
one inch wide. You begin by placing two strips of paper at
right angles to each other and by gluing the ends together,
one on top of the other. Now you fold the bottom strip up
and over the top strip, then the left strip over the right,
then the top over the bottom, then the right over the left,
and so on, as you can see in the diagrams.

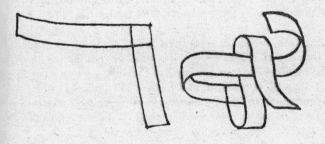

When you have got to the end of the strips of paper, glue
the ends together. When you loosen the paper, you will
find you've made a marvellous chain.

Frozen Pond and Milk Top Decorations

FROZEN POND

Find a small mirror and spread a little glue round the outside edge. Stick cotton wool onto the glue and fluff it up so that it looks like a snow-covered hedge surrounding a frozen pond. Stick one or two fir cones or bits of holly into the cotton wool to look like trees and stand one or two figures and perhaps some animals in the middle of the mirror. Sprinkle artificial snow over the mirror and you will have made an attractive Christmas scene.

MILK TOP DECORATIONS

With milk bottle tops, a pair of scissors, needle and thread, you can make lots of lovely decorations for the Christmas tree. An easy one to start with is a star. Begin by flattening out the milk top and drawing the shape of a star onto it. Cut out the star and thread a piece of cotton through the top.

To make a bell, press the edges of the milk top over your first finger. Be very careful or the edge of the milk top will cut you. Mould the milk top round your finger and make it curl up at the bottom to look like a bell. To hand it on to the tree, thread a piece of cotton through the middle.

CHRISTMAS CARDS & PRESENTS

Christmas Cards & Presents

A boy of twelve called William Egley is supposed to have invented the very first Christmas card in 1842. Before then, children had given their parents 'Christmas pieces' - coloured paper with Christmas greetings inscribed - but it was William Egley who set the fashion with his illustrated card. The idea caught on quickly. In 1843 the first Christmas cards were printed (just 1,000 of them, sold at one shilling or fivepence each) and over the years more and more cards have been produced until nowadays hundreds of millions of Christmas cards are sent through the post each December.

Of course, you can always buy Christmas cards, but they can be expensive and they are not nearly as nice to give or to receive as home-made cards. The same goes for presents. It is very nice to give your mother a book or some soap or a scarf, it is very nice to give your father some socks or some chocolate or a tie, it is very nice to give your brothers and sisters a magazine or a record or a poster, but it is much, much nicer to give them something you have made yourself.

Here are some ideas for home-made cards and home-made presents. They're all quite easy to make and there should be something here to appeal to most people.

Christmas Cards

The simplest way to make a Christmas card is to draw one.
Take a stiff piece of paper or card, fold it down the middle
and draw a picture on the front. Make the picture a
Christmassy one and draw a Nativity scene or a Christmas
tree or Father Christmas or a robin or a snow scene. On
the inside write HAPPY CHRISTMAS or MERRY
CHRISTMAS AND A HAPPY NEW YEAR in different
coloured pencils.

If you want to give your Christmas card a special shape,
make sure that you fold the paper along the top and draw a
shape that touches the fold. When you have drawn the
shape, cut it out and colour it.

If you don't like drawing, you can always make a card by
cutting out pretty shapes with tissue paper and sticking
them onto a card. A Christmas tree shape is a good idea and
if you let the different shapes overlap, and sprinkle some
glitter or artificial snow onto the card while the glue is still
drying, you can make a very pretty and original card.

If you want to make a Christmas card and present
combined, and you live in a fairly large town, you can
probably find an automatic machine where you can have
your photograph taken. It won't cost very much and you
can then glue your picture onto a card and draw a frame
around the picture. On the inside of the card, of course,
you write your Christmas greeting.

Book Covers

If you decide to buy a book as a present for a member of
your family, why not make a special cover for it as well?
Even if you don't want to buy the book, you can always
cover a book that the person to whom you are giving the
present already owns.

Making the cover is very easy. All you do is cut out a
piece of material about fifteen inches long by nine inches
wide (or more if it's a big book) and lay the book open on
top of the material. Now at each end, fold over the material
and glue it at the top and bottom like this:

Be very careful not to get any glue on the book itself. (If you
know how to sew, you can always use a needle and thread
instead of glue). And leave enough room to be able to slip
the book in and out of the cover when you want to.

If you enjoy reading and like having books, this is a good
present to give to yourself. It helps protect your books and
keep them clean

Bookmarks and Christmas Holders

BOOKMARKS

If you want to give a present to someone who enjoys reading books, you can always give them a bookmark. Cut out a piece of felt (or another material) about seven inches long and one inch wide and fray the bottom of it by making little snips with your scissors at one end. With a felt-tip pen write the name of the person to whom you are giving the present on one side of the bookmark.

CHRISTMAS HOLDER

All you need to make a handy holder for pencils and pens or pipes and pipe-cleaners or toothbrushes and combs is an old yoghurt carton, some scraps of material, a length of ribbon, glue and a pair of scissors.

Begin by cutting the bits of material into interesting and attractive shapes. Now glue the material onto the side of the empty yoghurt carton. Make sure it sticks firmly and don't worry if you let the material overlap. All you must <u>not</u> do is let any of the carton show through. When the bits of the material have all been glued into position, glue a length of colourful ribbon around the top of the carton to give it a neat and pretty edge. When that's done, the present's made.

Egg - Shell Mosaic and Jigsaw

EGG-SHELL MOSAIC

Draw a large picture on a piece of card and fill it in with bits of broken egg-shell. If you like you can paint the egg-shell first. Glue the little bits of egg-shell into position and don't be surprised if you need quite a few shells. (This is one of those presents to make on a day when the whole family has had omelettes for lunch).

The picture can be of anything you like, but two ideas that look good as egg-shell mosaics are a picture of a fish and a picture of Humpty Dumpty. The fish looks good because the bits of egg-shell look like a fish's scales and Humpty Dumpty looks good because, of course, he was an egg anyway.

JIGSAW

All you need to make a jigsaw are a pair of scissors and a picture - the bigger the better. An old Christmas card would do, or a picture postcard or better still, a colourful poster. Take the picture and cut it up into about twenty pices (more if you are going to give it to a grown-up and fewer if you are going to give it to a small child). Try to make the pieces all different shapes and sizes.

When you have finished cutting up the pieces, gather them all together and put them in an envelope. Because it will help whoever you give the jigsaw to, think of a title for the jigsaw and write it on the envelope.

Melon Seed Necklace and Paperweight

MELON SEED NECKLACE

You can buy melon seed necklaces in the shops and they are quite expensive. To make one will cost you almost nothing - but you will have to wait until you have a melon for lunch or supper and remember to keep all its seeds.

The seeds must be washed and dried before you can start to make the necklace. When they are ready, all you do is thread them onto a length of cotton. Be sure to tie a big knot in one end of the cotton before you start. When you have threaded enough seeds onto the cotton to make a necklace, tie the loose end of the cotton to the end with the knot in it. Now dip the necklace into a pot of colourful paint and hang it up to dry. When the paint has dried, you will have a lovely necklace and a splendid Christmas present.

PAPERWEIGHT

This is an easy present to make if you live near the sea-side. If you don't, it isn't, because you need lots of little shells and a large stone to work with. If you are good at planning things well in advance, you might be able to remember to collect some shells in the summer and keep them hidden until you are ready to make the present. It's worth trying to remember, because the shell-paperweight is a marvellous present to be able to give anyone.

Making it is simple. Take your stone, which should be fairly large and round and flat, and cover it with very strong glue (or a mix of Polyfilla if you have any in the house). Now stick onto the stone all the little shells and pebbles that will fit. Let it dry and, if you have any, spray it with varnish.

Mosaic

Begin by drawing a pattern on a piece of white paper. It can be any pattern you like: a circle, a square, a triangle, a cat, a mouse, a Christmas tree. It doesn't matter, so long as you like it. Now collect together lots and lots of tiny bits of paper, but make sure they are all the same colour. If green is the colour you have chosen, you'll want lots of little bits of green paper, some light green, some dark green, some emerald green, some with green stripes, some with green dots, some printed with green ink. You can use drawing paper, wrapping paper, crepe paper, tissue paper, newspaper and paper from magazines.

Once you have drawn your pattern and collected all your little bits of paper, fill the pattern with the paper, gluing in one piece at a time. Make sure you cover the whole pattern, leaving no white showing through and using all the different shades of green paper. When you have stuck on all the bits of paper and allowed the glue to dry, you will find you have created a very attractive mosaic.

Pencil Cover

If you want to give someone a present that's really useful, you can always give them a pencil. If you want to make the pencil look nice, you can always make a pretty pencil cover for it. To begin with you will have to buy the pencil and collect together a few odd scraps of material. The largest piece of material needs to be seven inches long and two inches wide.

Lay the large piece of material out on the table, place the pencil on top of it and roll the material round the pencil. Spread a little glue along one of the edges of the piece of material and glue it down. You have now made a little tunnel out of the material with the pencil sitting inside it. Glue down one end of the tunnel.

Now cut out two small circles of material (the top of an egg-cup will give you the right shape) and glue them together round the edge, putting a little cotton wool between the two to act as stuffing. If some of the stuffing sticks out at one place it will look like hair. Now cut out the shapes of eyes, noses and mouths and stick them onto each side of the two circles. Stick the two-sided face you've just made onto the closed end of the tunnel and you'll find you have made an amusing cover for the pencil.

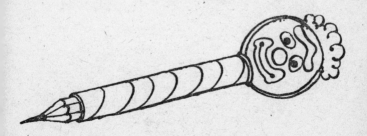

Tiny Tops

Often it's the simplest things that give most pleasure and
tiny tops, which are so simple to make, are presents that
always give fun. To make a tiny top, all you need to do is
draw a circle on a piece of card (use a tenpenny piece or the
top of an egg-cup to give you the shape) and put an old
matchstick you have sharpened to a point through the centre.
To make the top attractive, you can paint the matchstick
and the card.

CHRISTMAS FOOD

In days of old, the head of a wild boar was a favourite Christmas dish. You probably wouldn't want to serve it at your Christmas party, but in the past people used to eat the most extraordinary things at this time of the year - geese, swans, peacocks and pickled oysters to start with!

In Great Britain, people have been having turkey for their Christmas dinner since about 1540 and there was a time when the poor old turkeys had to walk all the way from Norfolk to London and set out months in advance to get to the capital city in time for Christmas day. Happily, that's a tradition that's lost and gone forever, but there is another tradition that is as strong as ever it was, pulling the wish-bone. If you have turkey or chicken at Christmas, you must take the wish-bone and pull it with a member of your family, wishing a wish as you pull. If you get the longer bit of the bone when it snaps, your wish will come true - providing you keep it a secret.

There's another tradition that says you must eat one mince pie on every one of the twelve days of Christmas. If you do, you are sure to have a happy twelve months ahead of you. Well, this book wants you to have just that, so there is a recipe for making twelve mince pies later in the chapter.

There are lots of other recipes as well and if you use them you should be able to prepare a splendid feast for your friends when they come to see you at Christmas. Some of the recipes are easier than others and it's very important to read the recipe right through before you start to cook. It's important too to have a grown-up with you if you are going to use any of the recipes where you will need to use a knife or turn on the oven.

Be sure before you begin to get all the bits and pieces you need around you. Wash your hands, put on an apron and clear your working surface before you start and if you've any doubts - about the measurements, about when something is boiling and when it isn't, about what the ingredients ought to be - check with a grown-up right away. If you leave it, you may be too late!

Chocolate Crispy Cakes

You will need:

Cornflakes or rice crispies
a bar of plain chocolate or milk chocolate or cooking chocolate
a mixing bowl
a saucepan
a spoon

The recipe:

Break the chocolate up into the mixing bowl and place the
bowl over a saucepan of <u>very hot</u> water on the stove and wait
until the chocolate melts. When the chocolate has melted,
remove the bowl and stir in the cornflakes or rice crispies.
When the rice crispies or cornflakes are thoroughly covered
in chocolate, put one spoonful at a time round a serving dish.
Each dollop will make an individual cake and will be ready
to eat in about ten minutes.

Chocolate Pudding

You will need:

3 rounded tablespoons of cornflour
3 rounded tablespoons of castor sugar
2 rounded tablespoons of cocoa powder
1 pint of milk
a few drops of vanilla essence
a saucepan
a mixing bowl
a serving bowl
a wooden spoon

The recipe:

Begin by putting the cornflour, the castor sugar and the cocoa powder into the mixing bowl. Add a little milk and mix it into a smooth paste. Put the rest of the milk into the saucepan and heat it. When it's very hot (but not boiling), pour it into the mixing bowl and stir well. Once it is mixed pour it all back into the saucepan, put the saucepan back on the heat and keep stirring until the mixture has thickened and is boiling. Now take the saucepan off the heat and stir in a few drops of vanilla essence. Pour the mixture into a serving bowl and serve it with cream or cold milk.

Chocolate Sauce for Ice Cream

You will need:

6 rounded tablespoons of castor sugar
4 rounded tablespoons of cocoa powder
¼ pint of water
a saucepan
a small bowl
a wooden spoon
a hand whisk

The recipe:

Begin by putting the water and the sugar into the saucepan
and then put the saucepan over a low heat. Stir until the
sugar has dissolved and then bring the water up to boiling
point (when it starts to bubble furiously, it's boiling), then
you let it simmer (on the edge of boiling) for one minute
and then take the saucepan off the heat. Add the cocoa
powder and whisk it until the sauce is smooth. Pour it into
the small bowl and leave it to cool, stirring it once in a while
until it thickens.

Now pour it all over your vanilla or chocolate ice cream.

Christmas Cup

You will need:

1 pint of cider
1 pint of lemonade
1 pint of undiluted orange squash
1 orange
1 apple
ice cubes
a large jug
a large spoon
a knife

The recipe:

Here's a Christmas Cup to serve your friends when you don't want tea (because you're tired of it), don't want orange squash (because you're bored with it), and don't want cola (because it rots your teeth). It makes a delicious party drink and it's got a bit of bite. Begin by pouring all the cider, lemonade and undiluted orange squash into the jug. Now wash the orange and cut it up into slices (including the peel). Wash the apple, take out the core and slice it too. Drop the sliced fruit into the jug and stir well. Add a few ice cubes and serve. You should have enough for a dozen party-goers.

Christmas Stars

You will need:

18 level tablespoons of flour
½ teaspoon of ground ginger
2 oz. of butter
2 tablespoons of brown sugar
2 level tablespoons of golden syrup
a knife or a star-shaped pastry cutter

a mixing bowl
a tablespoon
a teaspoon
a saucepan
a wooden spoon
a rolling pin
a sieve
2 baking trays
a skewer

The recipe:

Begin by pushing the flour and ginger through the sieve into the mixing bowl. Put the butter, the brown sugar and the golden syrup into the saucepan and heat the saucepan, stirring until the butter has melted. Now take the saucepan off the heat and pour the mixture onto the flour and mix it all up with the wooden spoon. When it is mixed and in a round ball take it out of the bowl and with a rolling pin roll it out thinly on the working surface. Cut it into the shapes of stars, using the knife or, if you've got one, a star-shaped pastry cutter. (Of course, you can make any other shape you like - a circle, a heart, a Christmas tree, whatever you think of). Lift the stars onto the baking trays which should be greased first. You can grease the trays by simply wiping them with the inside of the wrapping paper that was around the butter. If you think you would like to hang the stars from your real Christmas tree, make a little hole in one corner with a skewer (or a knitting needle!). Turn on the oven to a moderate heat, (that is 350ºF or Gas No. 4) and when it has had time to warm up, pop the stars in and bake them for about twelve minutes. Once you have taken them out and they have cooled, you can thread cotton through the holes and hang them on the tree.

47

Flapjacks

You will need:

2 oz. of butter
1 rounded tablespoon of golden syrup
1 rounded tablespoon of soft brown sugar
8 heaped tablespoons of porridge oats
a pinch of salt
a saucepan
a seven-inch cake tin
a wooden spoon

The recipe:

Begin by greasing the cake tin (you can do that with the paper the butter was wrapped in: simply wipe the buttery side of the paper round the inside of the tin) and put it ready by the oven. Then turn the oven on to a moderate heat (that is 350ºF or Gas No. 4) and leave it to warm up. Now measure the butter, syrup and sugar into a saucepan and place the saucepan over a low heat, stirring it occasionally with the wooden spoon until the butter has melted. Remove the pan from the heat and add the porridge oats and the pinch of salt. Mix it well and then spoon the mixture into the cake tin, spreading it out evenly. Put the cake tin into the hot oven and leave the mixture to bake for twenty minutes.

When the twenty minutes is up, take the cake tin out of the oven and divide the flapjack into eight or ten portions with a knife. Leave it to cool and then take the flapjack out of the tin and break it into eight or ten delicious little portions.

Jelly

You will need:

1 packet of jelly
hot and cold water
a heat-proof dish
a wooden spoon

The recipe:

Begin by breaking the jelly into pieces and putting the pieces into a heat-proof dish that will hold at least one pint of liquid. Now cover the jelly with very hot water and stir it gently until all the jelly has dissolved. Next add enough cold water to make a pint of liquid and put the jelly in a cold place (such as the refrigerator) until it sets. If you like, you can add pieces of fruit - strawberries, bits of orange, slices of banana - to the jelly before it sets.

Frosted Fruits

You will need:

Apples, pears, plums, grapes
1 egg white
some castor sugar
some greaseproof paper
a small paintbrush

The recipe:

Frosted fruits look lovely and taste delicious. Arranged on a
large plate or in a fruit bowl, they make very attractive table
decorations and are worth trying even if you don't think
they will all be eaten at the party. Certainly, everyone will
admire them.

Begin by washing and polishing the fruit. You will have to
be fairly gentle with the soft fruit - the plums and the
grapes - but you can give the hard fruits - the apples and
pears - a vigorous shine with a clean tea-towel.

Next get the 'frosting' ready. Put the egg-white in a small
bowl and whisk it gently with a fork. Sprinkle lots of castor
sugar onto the greaseproof paper. Now dip the paintbrush
into the egg-white and start painting a piece of fruit. Don't
paint it all over, but put on streaky lines of egg-white. Then
roll the fruit - or, in the case of the grapes, dip the whole
bunch - in the castor sugar and allow it to dry.

Marzipan Snowman

You will need:

½ lb. of ready-made marzipan
icing sugar
2 currants
1 cherry
blunt knife
rolling pin

The recipe:

Begin by sprinkling some icing sugar onto your working
surface. Now roll the marzipan into a flat, rectangular shape.
Now with the blunt knife outline the shape of the snowman.
When you are sure you've got the shape right, cut out the
snowman and press two currants in as his eyes. Cut the
cherry in half and use one half as his nose and the other
half, cut into quarters, as his mouth. Lay him on a dish
with other Marzipan Snowmen.

Mince Pies

You will need:

2 heaped tablespoons of mincemeat
8 oz. of frozen puff pastry
some milk
some flour
some icing sugar
a rolling pin
a 2½ inch round pastry cutter
a baking tray for twelve tartlets
a pastry brush
a pair of scissors

The recipe:

Sprinkle a little flour onto your working surface and, with
the rolling pin, roll the pastry out thinly. Using the 2½ inch
round pastry cutter, stamp out twenty-four small circles of
pastry and place half of them in the baking tray for twelve
tartlets. With a teaspoon put a small portion of the mincemeat
on top of each of the twelve pieces of pastry in the baking
tray. With a little water dampen the edges of the remaining
twelve circles of pastry and stick one on top of each portion
of mincemeat, pressing down the edges now to seal the pies.
With the scissors snip two slits on the top of each mince pie
and, with the pastry brush dipped in milk, brush each of the
pies in turn. Turn the oven on to hot (which is 400°F or
Gas No. 6) and pop the tray of pies into the oven for twenty
minutes or so, until they have turned a gorgeous golden
brown. Take them out of the oven, serve them and take a
bow.

Peppermint Creams

You will need:

1 egg-white
12 heaped tablespoons of icing sugar
a few drops of peppermint essence
a mixing bowl
a sieve
a fork
a knife and a knife board
a wooden spoon

The recipe:

Begin by pouring the egg-white into the mixing bowl and
whisk it with the fork until it's frothy. Now sift the icing
sugar through the sieve and mix about eight tablespoons of
it into the egg-white, beating it firmly. Add a few drops of
peppermint essence.

Now turn the sticky mixture out onto your working
surface and mix in the rest of the sieved icing sugar. Divide
the mixture in half and shape it into a long worm about an
inch thick. Then, using the knife and the knife board, cut
the mixture into little portions. If you like, use your fingers
to shape them into circles. Leave them for at least four hours
to set firm. You should end up with about thirty-five
delicious peppermint creams.

Sandwiches

You will need:

1 loaf of thinly sliced bread
butter

different fillings
a bread board
a bread knife
an ordinary knife

The recipe:

Begin by spreading butter onto one side of all the slices of bread. Next spread the filling of your choice onto half the slices of bread, and put the slices with just butter on them on top of the slices with filling on them. Cut each sandwich into four with the bread knife and, if you've got very fussy friends or want to give a very grand party, cut off the crusts as well.

You can fill sandwiches with all sorts of delicious fillings. Some - like honey or peanut butter or chocolate spread or tomato ketchup or marmite or jam or sandwich spread - come out of a jar, but there are lots of tasty fillings that you can prepare for yourself. If you like savoury sandwiches you can make very good fish fillings by opening a tin of sardines (or tuna or salmon), pouring off the oil carefully, emptying the sardines into a bowl and mashing them up with a fork, adding just a pinch of salt and a squeeze of lemon juice. If you like sweet sandwiches, you must try banana ones. All you do to make the filling is unzip a banana, put it in a bowl, mash it up with a fork, adding a teaspoon of sugar (for sweetness) and a teaspoon of lemon juice (to stop the banana from going brown).

Sandwiches are delicious with almost anything inside them - slices of ham, mashed-up boiled egg with a little water-cress, grated cheese, even pieces of chocolate! - so when you give a Christmas party, be sure to serve a mixture of sandwiches, with some savoury and some sweet.

CHRISTMAS
FUN & GAMES

Christmas
Fun & Games

Here is a collection of games to play, tricks to perform, quiz-questions to answer and carols to sing at your Christmas party.

Animal Snap

Get all the players to choose an animal and have a go at making their animal's noise. Someone will be a cow and moo, someone will be a cat and miaow, someone will be a duck and quack, someone will be a hen and cluck, and so on. When everyone has chosen their animal and practised their noise, deal out a pack of cards (or two packs if you've got more than six players) and give everyone the same number of cards.

Each player has his cards on the table face-downward in front of him, and players take it in turns to turn over one card at a time. When a card is turned up that matches any other card on the table, the two players who own the matching cards must make each other's animal noises. So if Jill (who is a dog) turns up an Ace and Jack (who is a pig) turns up an Ace as well, Jill must hoink and Jack must bark. The player who makes the right noise first wins <u>all</u> the cards that are face-upwards on the table. The first player to collect all the cards in the pack is the winner.

Beetle

Any number can play this party game. All you need are pieces of paper and pencils for each player and one dice. The aim of the game is to be the first player to draw a beetle, but you can only draw your beetle when you throw the right number for each part. You need a 6 to start and each time you throw a 6 you get an extra turn. These are the numbers you have to throw to get the different parts of the beetle's body:

6 - the body
5 - the head
4 - the arms
3 - the legs
2 - the eyes
1 - the nose and mouth

Of course, you can't draw a head until you have got a body to attach it too and you can't draw eyes until you've got a head to put them in. The first player to complete a beetle is the winner.

Christmas Carol

Away in a manger, no crib for a bed,
The little Lord Jesus laid down His sweet head.
The stars in the bright sky looked down where He lay,
The little Lord Jesus asleep on the hay.

The cattle are lowing, the Baby awakes,
But little Lord Jesus no crying He makes.
I love Thee, Lord Jesus, look down from the sky,
And stay by my side until morning is nigh.

Christmas Trick

THINK OF A CARD

The effect: You leave the room while your assistant lays out nine cards on the table and invites the audience to choose one. You then return to the room and when your assistant has pointed to each card in turn asking 'Is it this one?' you tell him and everybody else which one it is.

The explanation: One of the nine cards your assistant lays out must be the Nine of Hearts. He must also lay out the nine cards in the pattern of the heart emblems on the Nine of Hearts. When he is pointing to the different cards and asking you 'Is it this one?' he is careful when he gets to the Nine of Hearts to point to the position on the card that will show you the chosen card's position on the table.

Blind Man's Banquet

This is a very funny and a very messy game. Two people
play it at a time and they are both blindfolded and made to
sit on the floor facing each other. As well as blindholds they
should wear bibs and, to be on the safe side, it would be a
good idea to cover the floor with an old sheet.

Each player is given a spoon and a bowl of jelly and has
to feed the player sitting opposite him. Nobody wins this
game, but the players get faces full of sticky jelly and the
people watching get a lot of laughs.

Christmas Carol

I saw three ships come sailing in,
*   On Christmas day, on Christmas day,*
I saw three ships come sailing in,
*   On Christmas day in the morning.*

And what was in those ships all three,
*   On Christmas day, on Christmas day?*
Our Saviour Christ and His lady,
*   On Christmas day in the morning.*

Pray, whither sailed those ships all three,
*   On Christmas day, on Christmas day?*
O, they sailed into Bethlehem,
*   On Christmas day in the morning.*

And all the bells on earth shall ring,
*   On Christmas day, on Christmas day,*
And all the angels in Heaven shall sing,
*   On Christmas day in the morning!*

Christmas Trick

CAUGHT CARDS

The effect: This is a trick to perform when everyone is sitting round a table. Stand up and hold up an ordinary pack of cards so that the audience can see the bottom card, but you can't. Explain to them that by <u>feeling</u> the cards you can tell a court card - a Jack, Queen or King - from the other cards. Looking towards the ceiling, you go through the pack a card at a time telling the audience whenever you get to a court card.

The explanation: You have an assistant sitting near you in the audience and whenever you get to a court card he taps you gently on the foot.

Charades

No Christmas party is complete without this game. To play it, divide everybody into two teams and send one team out of the room to think of the word they are going to turn into a charade. Words with two or three syllables are best and the idea is that the team must act out each part of the word separately and then the whole word together, while the other team watches. When the charade has been performed, the team watching has to guess what the word was. If they get it right they score a point. Teams take it in turns to leave the room and think of the words to act out.

Some good words for charades are: carrot (because you can do <u>car</u> and <u>rot</u>), carpet (<u>car</u> and <u>pet</u>), cabbage (<u>cab</u> and <u>age</u>), woman (<u>whoa</u>! and <u>man</u>), kidnap (<u>kid</u> and <u>nap</u>), nobody (<u>no</u> and <u>body</u>), bargain (<u>bar</u> and <u>gain</u>), bedroom (<u>bed</u> and <u>room</u>), earwig (<u>ear</u> and <u>wig</u>), buttercup (<u>butter</u> and <u>cup</u>), dandelion (<u>dandy</u> and <u>lion</u>), snowdrop (<u>snow</u> and <u>drop</u>), football (<u>foot</u> and <u>ball</u>), knapsack (<u>nap</u> and <u>sack</u>), mushroom (<u>mush</u> and <u>room</u>), marigold (<u>marry</u> and <u>gold</u>), pansy (<u>pan</u> and <u>sea</u>), rocket (<u>rock</u> and <u>ate</u>) and fortune (<u>four</u> and <u>tune</u>).

If you are going to present a word with two syllables, you will need to act out three scenes. The first will show the first syllable, the second the next syllable and the third the word as a whole. If you want to make the charade easier you can use costumes and if you want to make it more difficult you can mime it and do everything in silence.

When each team has left the room five times and acted out five different words, the team with most points has won.

Christmas Trick

POUND AND PENCIL

The effect: This is a very good trick to perform if you are lucky enough to have been given a pound note for Christmas. If you haven't got a pound note, you must borrow one. Explain to your audience that the pound note is a very powerful one and that you will prove it to them if someone will lend you a pencil. Now all you do is get someone to hold the pencil while you strike it with the side of the pound note - and the pencil snaps in two.

The explanation: As you hold the pound note and bring it down onto the pencil you put your forefinger along the bottom of the note and hit the pencil sharply. If you do it quickly, no one will notice and your finger won't get hurt.

Christmas Carol

While shepherds watched their flocks by night,
   All seated on the ground,
The angel of the Lord came down,
   And glory shone around.

'Fear not,' said he (for mighty dread
   Had seized their troubled mind),
'Glad tidings of great joy I bring,
   To you, and all mankind.

'To you, in David's town, this day
   Is born of David's line
A saviour, who is Christ the Lord,
   And this shall be the sign:'

'The heavenly Babe you there shall find
   To human view displayed,
All meanly wrapped in swathing bands,
   And in a manger laid.'

Thus spake the seraph, and forthwith
   Appeared a shining throng,
Of angels, praising God, and thus
   Addressed their joyful song:

'All glory be to God on high,
   And to the earth be peace;
Good wil' henceforth from heaven to men
   Begin and never cease!'

Balloon Rockets

Give all the players an unblown-up balloon and get them to
stand along a straight line at one end of the room. One by
one get them to blow up their balloons and release them.
The air escaping from the balloons will make them rocket
across the room and whoever gets his balloon to travel
furthest is the winner.

Giddy Goats

All the players sit in a circle on the floor. One player begins by calling out the first letter of a word, the next player adds another letter, the next another. The word goes round the group and the player who finishes the word by adding the last letter has to get up, go 'Baa-baa!' and turn round on the spot six times. He is now out of the spelling part of the game and every time it comes to his turn he has to get up and revolve and go 'Baa-baa'.

Each time a word is ended, the player who said the last letter becomes a Giddy-goat, gets up, turns round on the spot six times and says 'Baa-baa', until, all but one of the players have become Giddy-goats. That one player is the winner.

Christmas Trick

NAME THE OBJECT

The effect: You leave the room and the others choose an object in the room. When you return you correctly name the object they have chosen.

The explanation: When you return to the room, your assistant points at different objects and asks if that was the object. Just before pointing to the chosen object, he will point to something black.

Christmas Carol

O little town of Bethlehem,
    How still we see thee lie;
Above thy deep and dreamless sleep
    The silent stars go by;
Yet in thy dark streets shineth
    The everlasting light;
The hopes and fears of all the years
    Are met in thee tonight.

How silently, how silently,
    The wondrous gift is given;
So God imparts to human hearts
    The blessings of His heaven:
No ear may hear His coming,
    But in this world of sin
Where meek souls will receive Him, still
    The dear Christ enters in.

O Holy Child of Bethlehem,
    Descend to us, we pray;
Cast out our sin and enter in,
    Be born in us today.
We hear the Christmas angels
    The great glad tidings tell:
O come to us, abide with us,
    Our Lord, Emmanuel.

Goody Two Shoes

Don't play this game if you've got holes in your socks or think any of the other players might have! You start by getting everyone to take off one of their shoes and throw it into a pile in the middle of the room. You then distribute the shoes at random, giving a girl's shoe to a boy and a boy's shoe to a girl where possible.

Players then have to go around trying to find their own shoe and trying to find the owner of the shoe they have been given. As soon as you have got rid of the shoe you were given and have found your own shoe and put it on, you sit on the floor and stay still. The last two players left standing are the loosers.

Christmas Trick

MAGIC PHOTO

The effect: You explain to the audience that you have
invented a new type of camera called a spoon and ask your
assistant to photograph a member of the audience with the
spoon while you leave the room. You go out and your
assistant takes the photograph using the spoon. You return,
look at the spoon and correctly name the person who has
been photographed.

The explanation: When you return to the room, your
assistant has adopted the exact pose of whoever it is he
photographed, so you simply glance at your assistant, look
around the room to find someone sitting or standing in exactly
the same way and name the person.

Blind Man's Buff

Like Charades, this is one of those traditional games that must be played at every Christmas party. One of the players is blindfolded, revolved three times and left to catch hold of any of the other players, who do their best to keep out of his way. When he manages to catch someone, he tries to guess who it is by feeling their face. If he succeeds, the caught player becomes the next blind man. If he fails, he is revolved once more and has to catch somebody else.

Jingle-Jangle

This is like Blind Man's Buff in reverse. All the players except one are blindfolded and they have to catch the one player who can see and who has to carry a bell. The first blindfolded player to catch the player with the bell, swaps his blindfold for the bell for the next round.

Christmas Trick

BURNT NAMES

The effect: You have as many blank slips of paper as there are members of your audience. You invite each member of the audience to give you the name of a famous person in turn and you write the names on the slips of paper. You then fold the slips, place them in a hat and invite a member of the audience to take out just one slip and hold onto it without looking at it. You now burn all the other slips. Having done so, you tell the audience what name is on the one slip that has not been burnt.

The explanation. When the names are called out by the members of the audience, you carefully note the first name and write it down on every single slip of paper. No matter which slip is taken from the hat, you will know what name is written on it.

Old Maid

This famous card game is a good one to play at a Christmas party because any number can play and the rules are very simple. Begin by taking the Queen of Spades out of an ordinary pack of cards. Now deal out the remaining fifty-one cards to the players. The players look at their cards and if they happen to have any pairs - two Aces or two Fives or two Kings - they put these pairs face-downwards on the table.

The player to the left of the dealer offers his cards face-downward to the player sitting on his left who takes one of the cards. If the new card gives him a pair, he puts it on the table. It is then his turn to offer his cards to the player sitting on his left. This goes on around the group until all the cards have been paired off and placed on the table. when one player will be left holding an odd Queen. That player is the Old Maid and has lost the game.

A Penny for your Thoughts

The effect: You invite a member of the audience to join you on the stage and give him an ordinary pack of playing cards to hold. You then ask another member of the audience to lend you a penny. The penny you give to the member of the audience who is holding the cards. You ask him to look at it carefully and hold onto it. You then ask him to give you the top four cards on the pack. These cards you lay out face-upwards on the table. You ask him to tell you the date on the penny he is holding and it turns out that the numbers on the cards and the date on the coin are the same.

The explanation: Before the trick you have chosen your own penny (a 1972 penny, for example) and sorted the cards so that the top four are an Ace, a Nine, a Seven and a Two. When it comes to performing the trick all you have to do is swap your penny for the one you are lent before passing it over to the member of the audience who is already on stage with you holding the pack of cards.

Merry Christmas

To play this game all the players must stand in a circle, holding hands. They then go round in groups, taking it in turns to count, from 1 to infinity - except that whenever a player gets to 5 or a multiple of 5 (like 10, 15, 20, 25, 30, 35 and 40), he mustn't say the number. He must say 'Merry Christmas' instead. So, with four players, this is how the first three rounds would go:

Player One:	1
Player Two:	2
Player Three:	3
Player Four:	4
Player One:	MERRY CHRISTMAS!
Player Two:	6
Player Three:	7
Player Four:	8
Player One:	9
Player Two:	MERRY CHRISTMAS!
Player Three:	11
Player Four:	12

Any player who says 5, or a multiple of 5, or who gets a number in the wrong order or who says 'Happy New Year' instead of 'Merry Christmas', drops out. The last player left counting is the winner.

Christmas Trick

MAGIC STRING

The effect: You show your audience an ordinary drinking straw and an ordinary piece of string. You thread the string through the straw, so that a little piece of string is sticking out of both ends of the straw. You then bend the straw in the middle, cut through it with a pair of scissors, but miraculously manage to produce the string unharmed and in one piece.

The explanation: On one side of the straw you cut a small slot and you make sure when you bend the straw to cut it, that the slot is on the underside. When the string is threaded into the straw, by pulling the ends of the string, you make sure that the string is drawn into the slot. As you cut the straw, you are able to avoid cutting the string.

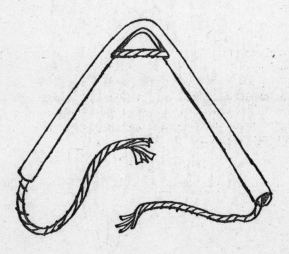

Christmas Carol

Hark! the herald angels sing
Glory to the new-born King;
Peace on earth and mercy mild,
God and sinners reconciled;
Joyful all ye nations rise,
Join the triumph of the skies,
With the angelic host proclaim,
Christ is born in Bethlehem.

Christmas Trick

THE GLASS OF WATER

The effect: Tell your audience that you can fill a glass with water and turn that glass upside down without spilling it. They won't believe you, but you can do it.

The explanation: Only half fill the glass and place a piece of paper on top of it. Now turn the glass upside-down very quickly. The water won't spill - but just to make sure, practise this trick over the bath or the kitchen sink a few times before performing it in public.

Bag Bursting

This is a noisy game that is great fun. Divide the players into two teams and line them up at one end of the room. At the other end of the room place two piles of empty paper bags. On the word 'Go!' the first player in each team runs forward, picks up a paper bag, blows it up and bursts it. When the bag has been burst, the player runs back to the starting line when the second member of the team sets off. The first team to have burst all its bags and have got back to the starting line wins the game.

Christmas Trick

OBEDIENT MATCHBOX

The effect: You place an ordinary matchbox on the back of your hand. When you tell it to stand up it does so. When you tell it to lie down it does so.

The explanation: Place the matchbox on the back of your hand face-down so that one end of the matchbox is just over your knuckles. Push the cover of the matchbox out slightly and when you close it again, catch a little bit of loose skin in between the tray of the matchbox and the cover. This way, when you clench your fist the skin on your hand will tighten and the box will stand up, and when you open your hand again the box will lie down.

Christmas Carol

O come all ye faithful,
Joyful and triumphant,
O come ye, O come ye to Bethlehem;
Come and behold Him,
Born the King of angels;
O come let us adore Him,
O come let us adore Him,
O come let us adore Him,
Christ the Lord.

Sing, choirs of angels,
Sing in exultation,
Sing, all ye citizens of heaven above,
Glory to God
In the highest;
O come let us adore Him,
O come let us adore Him,
O come let us adore Him,
Christ the Lord.

I Spy

One player starts the game by saying 'I spy with my little eye something beginning with A' - or B, or C, or D or any other letter. The other players must now guess what it is the first player is spying and the person who guesses correctly is the winner and becomes the next player to say 'I spy'.

It's important to remember that when you say 'I spy with my little eye', you must really be able to see whatever the mystery object is. And if you want to make it difficult for everybody else, you will choose an object which begins with a very common letter. After all, if you say 'I spy with my little eye something beginning with X' and there's a xylophone in the room, everyone is going to guess it at once, but if you say 'I spy with my little eye something beginning with T', the other players will take a long time to get the right answer because you could be thinking of so many things, television, toaster, tray, teapot, tie, tile, tissue, to mention just a few.

Christmas Quiz
Twenty Questions

1   Who made Christmas Trees popular in Great Britain:

   a) Prince Leopold?
   b) Prince Albert?
   c) Prince Charles?

2   Baron Hardup of Stoneybroke Hall had three daughters,
   Cinderella and her two Ugly Sisters. What was their
   servant called?

3   The Three Wise Men brought gifts for the baby Jesus.
   What were they?

4   The sixth of December is the Feast of Saint Nicholas.
   The twenty-sixth of December is another Saint's
   feast-day. Which one?

5   Aladdin's mother ran a Chinese laundry. What was her
   name?

6   When was the Christmas Card invented:

   a) in 1066?
   b) in 1735?
   c) in 1842?
   d) in 1945?

7   When is Twelfth Night?

8   *'On the first day of Christmas my true love sent to me'*
   'A partridge in a pear-tree'.
   What did he send on the second and third days?

9   Where was Dick Whittington when he heard the bells chime, 'Turn again Whittington, Lord Mayor of London'?

10   There is a famous carol about a good king who 'looked out on the Feast of Stephen, when the snow laid round about, deep and crisp and even'. What was the King's name and how do you spell it?

11   Name two of Father Christmas's reindeer.

12   Where was Jesus born? And where did he grow up?

13   Ilex aquifolium and Hedera helix are Latin names for two plants especially associated with Christmas. What are they?

14   Who wrote a book called 'A Christmas Carol' and who wrote a play called 'Twelfth Night?'

15   Fill in the blanks in the opening lines of this famous carol:

     'I saw BLANK BLANK come BLANK in,
     'On Christmas day, on Christmas day;
     'I saw BLANK BLANK come BLANK in,
     'On Christmas day in the BLANK.'

16   Robin Hood often appears in the pantomime story of Babes in the Wood. Name:

     a) One of his Merry Men.
     b) His great enemy.
     c) The girl he marries.

17   Here are the first two lines of a famous rhyme:

     'Christmas is coming, the geese are getting fat,
     'Please put a penny in the old man's hat'.

What are the next two lines?

18   Who sat in a corner eating a Christmas pie?

19   Captain Cook discovered Christmas Island in 1777.
      Where is it:

      a) in the Atlantic Ocean?
      b) in the English Channel?
      c) in the Pacific Ocean?
      d) in the Irish sea?

20   Unjumble these letters and make a seasonal greeting:

I AM SAD REACH MY STY NAPPY WE HEAR RNR

(See page 127 for answers)

A CHRISTMAS
NATIVITY
PLAY

Putting on a Nativity Play

Nativity plays have been performed in homes, in churches, in theatres, in market squares for hundreds of years. This Nativity play, like all the others that have gone before it, tells the story of the birth of Jesus and it has been written so that you can perform it at home with a few friends.

You need a cast of ten, but you can still put on the play if you have too many people or too few. If the Innkeeper also plays the part of the Angel and if you have only one Wise Man and one Shepherd, you can do it with six actors. And if you add on extra Shepherds and put some more animals in the stables and give the Sheperds some sheep to look after, you can use up to sixteen actors.

You don't need a proper stage and you don't need proper costumes. In fact, if you haven't got a room where the actors can come off and on when they are due to speak, you can have everyone in the acting area right from the beginning of the play. They must have their backs to the audience and keep perfectly still until it is their turn to appear, when they can turn round and start to speak or sing.

This is probably the best way to lay out the stage, particularly if all the actors are going to be on stage throughout:

	The Inn	
	The Stable	
LEFT SIDE	The Shepherds The Wise Men	RIGHT SIDE

Audience

Dress the characters as best you can. If you've got a dressing-up box, so much the better. If not, old clothes, old coats, scarves, sheets, blankets, eiderdowns - all will come in useful. Don't worry about girls playing boys' parts: if the acting is good it doesn't matter. The one thing that is important is that you learn your lines and rehearse the play several times before you show it to a proper audience.

The stage directions telling you when to move where are in brackets and the carols should be sung, but can be spoken if you haven't got a piano to accompany you and don't want to sing on your own.

The Nativity Play

(Enter JOSEPH and MARY from the right. They are very tired and JOSEPH has his arm around MARY. Slowly, wearily, they make their way towards the door of the Inn)

MARY: Oh, Joseph, I'm so tired. I don't think I can go a step further.

JOSEPH: Don't worry, dear. We're nearly there. We'll soon find somewhere to spend the night.

MARY: I hope so, I really hope so, because I can't go on. I'm quite exhausted.

JOSEPH: I know, but here's an inn that looks just right. I'm sure it will take us. I'll knock.

(He knocks on the door)

JOSEPH: Funny, nobody's answering. I'll try again.

(He knocks again. A voice is heard from inside the Inn)

INNKEEPER: Sorry! No room!

MARY: Oh no, they must have a room.

JOSEPH: I'll knock again.

(He does so and the door is opened a moment later by the Innkeeper. He is very angry)

INNKEEPER: Didn't you hear me? I said 'No room!'

JOSEPH: Oh, yes, we heard you, but you see, we're desperate. We've come all the way from Nazareth and we're exhausted -

INNKEEPER: All the way from Nazareth? You can't have! It's hundreds of miles.

JOSEPH: It is a long way and we are so tired.

INNKEEPER: Well, I'm very sorry, but we're full and thats that. You'd better try somewhere else.

JOSEPH: We've tried everywhere we've passed and they say they're all full too.

INNKEEPER: Well, I can't help that. Now, if you'll excuse me, I've got to get back to my guests. They want their food and drink.

MARY: But it's so bitterly cold out here.

INNKEEPER: That's what comes of travelling in the middle of winter. You shouldn't do it.

JOSEPH: But we had to come to Bethlehem to register our names for the census. Please help us.

INNKEEPER: Sorry, nothing doing. Good-night!

(He goes back into the Inn and closes the door. JOSEPH knocks again)

JOSEPH: I'll tell him about the baby. He must help us. We've got nowhere else to go.

(The INNKEEPER opens the door. He is very angry now)

INNKEEPER: For the last time, go away! I'm full up and I'm fed up - and if you don't clear off, I'll kick you off the doorstep. Do you understand me?

JOSEPH: But my wife is going to have a baby and it's so cold out here.

INNKEEPER: Well, it's not my fault.

JOSEPH: I know that, but all she wants is a roof over her head, just for tonight. Haven't you got anywhere we could go?

INNKEEPER: No!

MARY: What about the stable?

INNKEEPER: Well, what about the stable?

MARY: Couldn't we sleep there?

INNKEEPER: The stable? Well, I don't see why not. You'll have to ask the cow, mind you! I don't think she'll mind though. No, you go and sleep in the stable - and give me a bit of peace and quiet. Good night!

(And he closes the door on them)

JOSEPH: Well, it's better than nothing. Come, let's have a look.

(They go to the stable)

JOSEPH: Well, it's not going to be very cosy.

MARY: I know, but at least we'll have a roof over our heads.

JOSEPH: A pretty leaky roof by the look of it.

MARY: Never mind.

JOSEPH: And here's the cow he told us about.

COW: Moo!

MARY: I hope she won't mind if we share her straw.

JOSEPH: You don't mind, do you cow?

(The COW shakes her head)

MARY: Well, that's very friendly of you. Thank you very much.

(The COW comes up to MARY and rubs itself up against her in a friendly way)

94

JOSEPH: I must say, she is friendly. I think we'll all get on very well, don't you?

(The COW moos and MARY laughs)

JOSEPH: Well, it's way past my bedtime, I think we ought to settle down.

MARY: I can't wait to get to sleep. I'm so tired.

(They settle down by the COW and begin to doze off)

JOSEPH: Sleep well, my dear, sleep well.

MARY: Thank you, Joseph. You sleep well too.

JOSEPH: I wonder if the baby will be born tonight.

MARY: I wonder.

JOSEPH: Good-night, Mary.

MARY: Good-night, Joseph.

JOSEPH: Good-night, Cow.

COW: Moo.

(They all fall asleep and lie there perfectly still. It is now the turn of the two SHEPHERDS on the left of the stage to come to life They are sitting cross-legged on the ground playing cards)

1st SHEPHERD: Snap!

2nd SHEPHERD: What do you mean, 'Snap'? That's a Jack, not a King, you idiot.

1st SHEPHERD: Oh, yes, you're right. Sorry.

(They carry on playing)

2nd SHEPHERD:	I don't like playing with cheats, but out here in the fields with nothing but a bunch of sheep I haven't got much choice. SNAP!
1st SHEPHERD:	All right, you win!
2nd SHEPHERD:	That means you owe me ninepence.
1st SHEPHERD:	Which proves I don't cheat. If I did, you be owing me money!
2nd SHEPHERD:	Fancy another game?
1st SHEPHERD:	Okay. You deal.

(While he is dealing, the ANGEL quietly appears behind the SHEPHERDS and taps the 2nd SHEPHERD on the shoulder. He jumps with fright and throws the cards all over the place)

2nd SHEPHERD:	Goodness, you gave me a fright!
1st SHEPHERD:	Who are you?
2nd SHEPHERD:	Yes, who are you? What are you doing here in the middle of the night?
1st SHEPHERD:	And dressed up like a silly angel.
ANGEL:	I am an angel.
BOTH SHEPHERDS:	You're what?!
ANGEL:	I am an angel and I have come to you to bring you the best news in the world.
2nd SHEPHERD:	What, have I won the Pools?
ANGEL:	No, it's nothing like that. It's something much more exciting. In the village of Bethlehem, just two miles from here, a child has been born tonight, a child who is the son of God.

1st SHEPHERD: What's his name?

ANGEL: His name is Jesus and you will find him lying in a manger in a stable.

2nd SHEPHERD: And how will we find the stable?

ANGEL: Do you see that star in the sky?

2nd SHEPHERD: The very bright one?

ANGEL: Yes, the very bright one. Follow it and it will lead to the stable.

1st SHEPHERD: Come on, let's go.

2nd SHEPHERD: We ought to take a present really.

1st SHEPHERD: All right, let's take one of the lambs. He'll like that.

2nd SHEPHERD: Yes, that's a good idea. But come on, we'd better hurry.

(One of the SHEPHERDS picks up a lamb. If you have only a few actors it can be a pretend-lamb, but if someone can act the part of the lamb he should be led by one of the SHEPHERDS. As they walk slowly towards the stable followed by the ANGEL, they sing this famous carol)

SHEPHERDS: Silent night, holy night!
All is calm, all is bright,
Round yon Virgin Mother and Child!
Holy Infant so tender and mild,
Sleep in heavenly peace,
Sleep in heavenly peace.

Silent night, holy night!
Shepherds first saw the light,
Heard resounding clear and long
Far and near the angel song;
Christ the Saviour is here,
Christ the Saviour is here.

(They have now reached the stable and find MARY sitting with the baby Jesus in her arms, with JOSEPH sitting on one side of her and the COW on the other. All of them sing the last verse of the carol together)

> ALL: Silent night, holy night!
>   Son of God, oh how bright
>   Love is smiling from Thy face,
>   Peals for us the hour of grace;
>   Christ our Saviour is born,
>   Christ our Saviour is born.

(When the carol is over, MARY, JOSEPH, the ANGEL, the COW and the SHEPHERDS remain quite still, while it becomes the turn of the three Wise Men, MELCHIOR, CASPAR and BALTHAZAR, to come to life)

MELCHIOR: The star is shining as brightly as ever. We'll be there before long.

CASPAR: I can hardly wait, Melchior. This is going to be the most exciting moment of my life.

BALTHAZAR: It's been a long journey Caspar, but worth every mile.

MELCHIOR: Look, Balthazar, the star is just overhead now.

BALTHAZAR: We must have arrived.

CASPAR: But where is the baby?

(MELCHIOR suddenly notices the stable)

MELCHIOR: There is the baby!

(As they advance towards MARY and JOSEPH and the baby Jesus, they sing a carol. When each one gets to his own verse, he kneels down and presents his gift. At the end of each verse all three sing the chorus)

98

ALL THREE: We three Kings of Orient are,
            Bearing gifts we travel afar,
            Field and fountain, moor and mountain,
            Following yonder star.

CHORUS: O star of wonder, star of night,
            Star with royal beauty bright,
            Westward leading, still proceeding,
            Guide us to Thy perfect light.

MELCHIOR: Born a King on Bethlehem's plain,
            Gold I bring to crown Him again.
            King forever, ceasing never,
            Over us all to reign.

CASPAR: Frankincense to offer have I,
            Incense owns a Deity nigh,
            Pray'r and praising, all men raising,
            Worship Him, God most high.

BALTHAZAR: Myrrh is mine, its bitter perfume,
            Breathes a life of gathering gloom.
            Sorrowing, sighing, bleeding, dying,
            Seal'd in the stone-cold tomb.

ALL THREE: Glorious now behold Him arise,
            King and God and Sacrifice,
            Alleluia, alleluia,
            Earth to heaven replies.

(The ANGEL who is standing behind MARY speaks)

ANGEL: These wise men have travelled many miles
            to see the baby Jesus, these good shepherds
            have left their flocks to see the baby Jesus.
            We have all come to this humble stable
            because this little baby is someone so
            special: he is the Son of God. And in many
            years to come, around the world, people
            will tell the story of what happened here in
            Bethlehem on the very first Christmas Day.

(Everyone, including the audience, now joins in singing the last carol)

EVERYONE: The first Noel, the angel did say,
Was to certain poor shepherds in fields
   as they lay,
In fields where they lay keeping their sheep
On a cold winter's night that was so deep.

CHORUS: Noel, Noel, Noel, Noel,
Born in the King of Israel.

They look-ed up and saw a star,
Shining in the East beyond them far,
And to the earth it gave great light,
And so it continued both day and night.

And by the light of that same star
Three wise men came from country afar;
To seek for a King was their intent,
And to follow the star wherever it went.

This star drew nigh to the north-west,
O'er Bethlehem it took its rest,
And there it did both stop and stay,
Right over the place where Jesus lay.

Then entered in those wise men three
Fell reverently upon their knee
And offered there, in His presence,
Their gold and myrrh and frankincense.

Then let us all with one accord,
Sing praises to our heavenly Lord,
That hath made heaven and earth of nought,
And with His blood mankind hath bought.

A CHRISTMAS PANTOMIME

Putting on a Panto

The Christmas Pantomime is a very British kind of fun. Its
history owes a lot to the Greeks and the Romans, the
Italians and the French, but today you won't find anything
quite like a pantomime outside England and Wales and
Scotland and Ireland. Panto is special to us.

'Cinderella' is the most popular of all the tradional
pantomime stories and, like almost all the others, it is simply
a very old fairy-tale with a happy ending. In different
countries there are different versions of the story. When they
tell the story in Rumania, for example, Cinderella isn't the
youngest daughter of Baron Hardup of Stoneybroke Hall at
all. She's an Emperor's daughter who is forced to live in a
pig-sty! And in Sweden, she is helped not by a fairy
Godmother, but by a kindly ox who gives her beautiful
clothes and carries her to court on his back.

We've told the story the British way and it's the way you
will see it if you go to see the pantomime of 'Cinderella' in
the theatre. If you want to put it on at home, it's not
difficult. You only need six people to play all the parts, and
while Buttons ought be to acted by a boy and Cinderella
and the Fairy Queen ought to be acted by girls, the parts of
the Prince and Clorinda and Thisbe, the Ugly Sisters, can be
played by boys or girls. In fact, one of the old pantomime
traditions is that the hero, who is called the Principal
Boy (in this case the Prince), is played by a girl actress dressed
up as a boy, and the laughable old lady, who is called the
Dame (in this case there are two dames: the Ugly Sisters) is
played by a man dressed up like a woman.

If you want to put on this pantomime at home, you must
read it through several times before you start and work out
all the moves. You must make sure that everyone learns their
lines and have lots of rehearsals before you put on a public
performance.

You won't need much scenery. In fact, for the kitchen at Stoneybroke Hall you only <u>need</u> a chair, but you can add all sorts of extra bits and pieces as well. A table, a fireplace, a broom for Cinderella, some pots and pans, a pumpkin in the corner, will all help make the scene look more real. For the Ballroom at the Palace, you don't really need any scenery at all, but it is important that you get someone to ring a bell or make a noise that will sound like a clock striking twelve.

The costumes are easy too. You can make them as grand or as simple as you like and your dressing-up box will allow. Cinderella should wear a simple shirt to begin with and a pretty party dress when she goes to the ball. The Ugly Sisters should look as ridiculous as possible, the Prince should look as smart as he can and Buttons can wear something simple (like a boiler-suit) throughout. The Fairy Queen should wear a pretty dress and, if possible, a pair of fairy wings.

Putting on a pantomime at home is great fun, but don't forget it does mean <u>a lot of hard work!</u>

Cinderella

Scene One: **THE KITCHEN**
AT STONEYBROKE HALL

(CINDERELLA is discovered sitting by the fireside looking miserable)

CINDERELLA: Oh dearime, I'm so hungry. And I don't know what to do. My sisters, Clorinda and Thisbe, are so cruel to me. They make me work all day and half the night. I have to get up at before five in the morning to start my chores. I've got to do everything for them - wash their clothes, polish their shoes, clean their rooms, cook their meals. I wouldn't mind, but they're always so rude to me as well. If Father was here he'd put a stop to it, but ever since Mother died he's been up in town trying to make enough money to keep his daughters in style. I'm so unhappy. When I'm not working, I just sit here in my rags by the fire, crying a little and dreaming about the fairy-tale Prince who will one day come and ask me to be his wife. But it's just a dream and I know I'm going to spend the rest of my life here, unhappy and alone. I've got nothing and no one.

(BUTTONS has just come in)

BUTTONS: You've got me!

CINDERELLA:	Of course, I have Buttons. How silly of me. How could I ever forget you?
BUTTONS:	I'm pleased to hear you say that, Miss Cinders. Because I'm you're friend you know. In fact, if I may make so bold, I'm probably the only friend you've got.
CINDERELLA:	That's true, Buttons.
BUTTONS:	And, by Jiminy, you need a friend living here all on your own with those two battle-axes.
CINDERELLA:	Really, Buttons, you mustn't call them that! They are my sisters, after all.
BUTTONS:	They're not very sisterly sisters if you ask me.
CINDERELLA:	Now, don't be naughty.
BUTTONS:	And why not, may I ask? I think you're too good to them. You shouldn't put up with them. I know I'm only the skivvy round here. I know I don't count for anything, but take my advice, Cinders. Stand up to those two. Tell them what you you think of them. Be firm. Be positive. They're a couple of nasty old frumps and it's high time you came out and said so.
CLORINDA *(off-stage)*:	CINDERELLA!
BUTTONS:	Oh, crikey, here they come! I'm off!

(BUTTONS goes off to the right and CLORINDA and THISBE, the Ugly Sisters, come in from the left)

CLORINDA:	Ah, Cinderella, here you are.
THISBE:	Sitting around doing nothing as usual, I see.

105

CLORINDA:	Lazy child.
CINDERELLA:	Oh, sisters, I'm so sorry. I was only taking a little rest before making the supper.
THISBE:	'A little rest'?! You must be joking! What does a strapping great horse of a girl like you need with 'a little rest'.
CINDERELLA:	Oh, I hope I'm not a strapping great horse of a girl.
CLORINDA:	Of course you are, child. Now don't take offence. The truth never hurt anybody.
THISBE:	Don't think we blame you. It's not your fault you're as plain as a pineapple and as simple as a sardine.
CLORINDA:	Just as it's not our fault that we're the greatest beauties for miles around.
THISBE:	I wouldn't say 'we' if I were you, Clo. I think it is generally acknowledged that I am the greatest beauty in this part of the kingdom.
CLORINDA:	Rubbish! You're not bad - for your age! - but when it comes to true beauty, you can't beat the real thing.
THISBE:	True beauty? Tush! Mutton dressed up as lamb.
CINDERELLA:	Sisters, sisters, don't fight!
CLORINDA:	You're right, child, it's not right to have fights within the family. Besides my health can't take it. I'm such a delicate thing.
THISBE:	Delicate! My foot!
CINDERELLA:	Now don't start all over again.

106

CLORINDA: Yes, don't start all over again. At the best of times I'm weak, but after this morning's breakfast I feel I'm knocking at Death's door.

CINDERELLA: Was something wrong with breakfast?

CLORINDA: Wrong? My dear child, you were never a good cook, but today you excelled yourself. As you know, I like my eggs boiled for precisely three minutes, not a second more, not a second less. Today my eggs must have been boiled for a least three minutes and a half. It isn't good enough.

THISBE: No, it really isn't. Your standards are dropping, girl. I think we'll have to teach you a lesson. You'll get no wages this week.

CINDERELLA: But I don't get any wages anyway.

CLORINDA: Quite right too.

THISBE: If we had our way, you'd pay us for the privilege of living in such charming company.

CINDERELLA: But I'm your sister.

THISBE: Yes, aren't you the lucky one!

CINDERELLA: Oh sisters, I promise I'll try to be better in future.

CLORINDA: That's more like it. Well you can get cracking right away and give me something to drink.

THISBE: I feel just like a cup of tea.

(BUTTONS enters)

BUTTONS: That's right – sloppy, wet and hot!

THISBE: You cheeky brat. How dare you speak to me like that?

CLORINDA: What are you doing in here, anyway?

BUTTONS: I've come to tell you that there's a fellow at the door who wants to come in.

THISBE: It'll be the police!

CLORINDA: No, it won't, it'll be the tax-collector.

CINDERELLA: It isn't someone with news from father, is it?

BUTTONS: No, it's a fellow called Dandini. He says he's the Prince's valet!

CINDERELLA:⎫
CLORINDA:⎬ The Prince's valet!
THISBE:⎭

CLORINDA: Show him in, show him in!

THISBE: At last, at last, the moment I've been waiting for!

CLORINDA: What do you mean, the moment you've been waiting for?

THISBE: Well, the Prince has obviously seen my picture in the local paper and decided I'm the one who should be his bride. He's looking for a wife you know.

CLORINDA: I know he's looking for a wife, but he's not looking for you. He could go to the zoo if he wanted to see the likes of you. It's the likes of me he's after!

THISBE: Poppycock!

CLORINDA: How dare you! I'll tear your eyes out!

108

(They are at each other's throat, when BUTTONS who had gone to fetch Dandini returns)

BUTTONS: The Prince's valet!

(Enter the PRINCE, disguised as his valet, Dandini. He bows to the Ugly Sisters, but doesn't notice CINDERELLA who is hidden behind them)

CINDERELLA
(aside): This is the Prince of my dreams! Can it be true?

PRINCE: Ladies this is indeed a pleasure.

CLORINDA: You're too kind, I'm sure, Mr. Bebeano.

PRINCE: Dandini's the name, madam.

THISBE: Of course, it is, I knew that. Ignore her, your valetship.

PRINCE: Let me get straight down to business.

CLORINDA:
THISBE: } Yes, yes?

PRINCE: I am here on behalf of His Majesty, the Prince -

CLORINDA:
THISBE: } Yes, yes?

PRINCE: To invite you -

CLORINDA:
THISBE: } To be his ever-loving wife!

PRINCE: Not at all, far from it. Whatever put that idea into your heads?

CLORINDA: I'm so sorry, to be sure.

THISBE: Carry on, carry on.

PRINCE: To invite you to his grand Ball which is
being given at his Palace tonight.

CLORINDA: Delighted. I accept.

THISBE
(aside): Once the Prince sees me, he'll want me as
his wife. He'd be a fool not to.

CLORINDA
(aside): As soon as the Prince sets his eyes on me
and all my loveliness, he'll ask me to marry
him at once. He'd be mad if he didn't.

THISBE: I accept too.

PRINCE: Well, I'm glad you can both come. Now
what about your younger sister?

CLORINDA:
THISBE: } What?

PRINCE: Your younger sister?

CLORINDA:
THISBE: } Who?

PRINCE: She is to be invited as well.

CLORINDA: But we haven't got a younger sister.

THISBE: Well, not so as you'd notice, anyway.

BUTTONS: Yes, they have and here she is!

*(BUTTONS steps forward and drags CINDERELLA with
him. The PRINCE gasps)*

PRINCE
(aside): But she is beautiful! This is the girl I've
dreamed of marrying!

BUTTONS: This is Baron Hardup's youngest daughter,
Cinderella.

(CINDERELLA curtseys)

110

PRINCE: Miss Cinderella, you too must come to the
              ball tonight. The Prince especially wishes
              it.

CINDERELLA: Thank you, kind sir.

PRINCE: Now, I must be on my way. I have all the
              great houses in the district still to visit. You
              must excuse me, ladies. Good day.

*(The PRINCE goes out the way he came in, followed by
BUTTONS)*

CINDERELLA: Invited to the Ball, me? It's too good to be
              true.

CLORINDA: You're right there, child. Going to the
              Ball's far too good for the likes of you.

THISBE: Yes, the Prince doesn't want an ordinary
              char at his party. He wants ladies of grace
              and refinement and exquisite beauty - like
              me!

CLORINDA: And me!

THISBE: Come on, sister, we must go and put on
              our ball gowns. If we're to be the belles of
              the Ball, we'd better get to work right
              away.

CLORINDA: Back to work, Cinders. We're off to the
              Ball!

*CLORINDA and THISBE go off to the left, leaving
CINDERELLA alone)*

CINDERELLA: Oh, I do so want to go to the Prince's Ball,
              but how can I? I've got nothing to wear, but
              these rags? My sisters won't let me travel
              with them and it's far too far to walk. I
              thought it was too good to be true.

111

(CINDERELLA sits by the fireside, dejected. The FAIRY QUEEN suddenly appears)

FAIRY QUEEN: Sweet Cinderella, have no fear - Your Fairy Godmother is here!

CINDERELLA: Am I dreaming?

FAIRY QUEEN: Of course not, my dear. I'm sorry if I startled you. I've only come to help.

CINDERELLA: But how can you help?

FAIRY QUEEN: You want to go to the Prince's Ball tonight?

CINDERELLA: Yes, but I've nothing to wear.

FAIRY QUEEN: Don't worry. My fairy power can turn those rags into the loveliest dress you ever saw. And my magic wand will turn a pumpkin into a fairy carriage and small white mice into fine white horses. You shall go to the Ball tonight!

CINDERELLA: Oh, thank you, thank you, thank you!

FAIRY QUEEN: But one thing you must remember. At the stroke of midnight my fairy power ends and you must leave the Ball by then or your coach and horses will disappear and your beautiful dress will turn back into rags.

CINDERELLA: I'll be good, I promise.

FAIRY QUEEN: Come Cinderella, come one and all, Let's make our way to the Prince's Ball.

END OF SCENE ONE

Scene Two: **THE BALLROOM**

AT THE PALACE

(CLORINDA and THISBE are with the PRINCE)

CLORINDA: Oh, Prince, you are <u>awful!</u>

THISBE: But I like you!

CLORINDA: Fancy pretending to be your valet, Bebeano -

PRINCE: Dandini.

CLORINDA: That's what I meant. Fancy pretending to be your valet, Danbeano, when you were the Prince all the time.

THISBE: You are a one!

CLORINDA: Would you care for a dance, Your Highness?

THISBE: Yes, would you care for a dance?

CLORINDA: I asked first.

THISBE: Yes, but I'm prettier.

CLORINDA: Stuff and nonsense.

(The PRINCE coughs)

PRINCE: Ladies, ladies, please!

THISBE: Forgive her, Prince, she's so ill-bred.

CLORINDA: Don't pay any attention to her, Your Highness. She can't help it you know.

THISBE: Poor dear, she's so old she's forgotton what manners are!

113

CLORINDA:	Oh, I could bite you!
THISBE:	Yes, you could - if you hadn't left your teeth at home! Ha! Ha!
PRINCE:	Girls!
CLORINDA: THISBE:	Yes?
PRINCE:	You're giving me a headache.
CLORINDA: THISBE:	Forgive her!
PRINCE:	Perhaps you would be kind enough to fetch me a glass of water. I think it might do my headache good.
CLORINDA: THISBE:	Of course, I'll get it!
CLORINDA:	No, I'll get it.
THISBE:	Let me get it. I have a way with water.
PRINCE:	Why don't you both go and get it.
CLORINDA: THISBE:	Oh, all right. Bye bye for now.

(And off they go to get the PRINCE'S water)

PRINCE:	Alone, at last. Now to find that beautiful girl I danced with a few moments ago. Look, here she comes.

(Enter CINDERELLA)

PRINCE:	Fair lady, what is your name?
CINDERELLA:	That is a secret, sir. What is yours?
PRINCE:	I am the Prince.

CINDERELLA
   (aside):   So he's not Dandini!

   PRINCE: And I'd like you to be my Princess.

CINDERELLA: Oh, but Your Highness -

(The Clock begins to strike twelve)

   PRINCE: Will you say yes?

CINDERELLA: I, I -

   PRINCE: Yes?

CINDERELLA: I must fly!

(She runs off stage as the clock strikes twelve)

PRINCE: Lady, sweet lady, come back!

(Enter CLORINDA and THISBE. CLORINDA is carrying a glass of water. THISBE is carrying a glass slipper)

CLORINDA:⎫
THISBE:⎭ We're back!

PRINCE: Did you pass anyone on the way?

CLORINDA: As a matter of fact we did. Some sort of serving girl. She almost knocked me over.

THISBE: Rude thing!

CLORINDA: Never mind, I've brought you your glass of water.

THISBE: And I've brought you this glass slipper. We found it on the way.

PRINCE: Her slipper! Give it to me. I shall search the land, I shall search the world, and whoever's foot shall fit this glass slipper shall be my bride.

CLORINDA: Well, this is quite a turn-up for the books.
THISBE: The Prince falling for a slipper - and ignoring our good looks!

END OF SCENE TWO

(CINDERELLA and BUTTONS are discovered by the fireside)

BUTTONS: Well, Cinders, did you have a good time last night?

CINDERELLA: Oh, I did, Buttons, I did.

BUTTONS: Did you meet the Prince.

CINDERELLA: Yes, I did, and you'll never believe it, but he asked me to marry him.

BUTTONS: He didn't!

CINDERELLA: He did!

BUTTONS: And did you say 'Yes'?

CINDERELLA: No.

BUTTONS: Phew! That's a relief, because you know, Cinders, I want to marry you myself.

CINDERELLA: But I didn't say 'No'.

(There is a knock at the door)

BUTTONS: I'd better go.

(BUTTONS goes to answer the door and CLORINDA and THISBE enter from the other direction)

CLORINDA: Standing about doing nothing, as usual, I see.

THISBE: I don't know who you think you are, Cinderella. Lady Muck? You can't spend all day every day idling about.

CLORINDA: Go and get on with your work, child.

THISBE: Go on! Shoo!

(CINDERELLA goes off)

CLORINDA· Oh, she's a lazy girl.

THISBE: Dreadful! If only she wasn't our sister, we could give her the sack.

(Enter BUTTONS and the PRINCE)

BUTTONS: His Royal Highness, the Prince!

PRINCE: Good morning, ladies.

CLORINDA: How sweet of you to call so soon, Prince.

THISBE: The answer's 'Yes', by the way, Prince.

PRINCE: Yes - what?

THISBE: Yes, I will marry you.

CLORINDA: Oh no you won't.

THISBE: Oh, yes I will.

CLORINDA: Oh, no you won't.

THISBE: Oh, yes I will.

PRINCE: Ladies, please -

BUTTONS: Belt up!

PRINCE: I will marry one of you -

CLORINDA:⎫
THISBE:⎭ Oh!

PRINCE: If this slipper fits.

THISBE: Don't worry, it will!

CLORINDA: Hand it over, I'll try it on first.

THISBE: No you won't, I'll go first.

CLORINDA: Me first!

BUTTONS: Prince, why don't you let
the older of the two sisters try it on
first?

PRINCE: What a good idea. Which one of you
should be first?

THISBE: Not me, Your Highness, not me.

CLORINDA: Of course, it should be her. She's years
and years and years older than I am, I'm
a mere child.

THISBE: You're an old fossil!

PRINCE: Now stop arguing and come over here.

*(THISBE goes to the PRINCE who kneels down and tries
to fit the slipper onto her right foot)*

THISBE: It fits! It fits!

PRINCE: What do you mean 'It fits!'? I can't even
get your toes in, never mind you heel.

THISBE: Well, I didn't want to marry you anyway.

CLORINDA: Sour grapes, eh? Well, sister, watch me.

*(CLORINDA goes to the PRINCE who tries to fit the
slipper onto her foot)*

CLORINDA: Ow!

PRINCE: What's the matter?

CLORINDA: I've got warts on the ends of my toes!

PRINCE: Warts or no warts, the slipper doesn't fit.

CLORINDA: Silly slipper!

PRINCE: Are there any other ladies in the house?

THISBE: We're the only ones.

PRINCE: Are you sure?

CLORINDA:
THISBE: } Yes!

BUTTONS: They're lying, Your Majesty.

CLORINDA:
THISBE: } Oh no we're not.

BUTTONS: Oh yes you are - and I'll prove it.

(BUTTONS rushes off)

CLORINDA: Cheeky scamp!

THISBE: Impudent rascal!

(BUTTON returns with CINDERELLA)

BUTTONS: Your Highness, this is Cinderella.

PRINCE: I think we've met before. Cinderella, let me see if this glass slipper fits you, because if it does I will ask you to be my bride.

(The PRINCE kneels at CINDERELLA'S feet and tries on the slipper)

PRINCE: It fits!

BUTTONS: Hooray!

CLORINDA:⎫
THISBE:⎬ Boo!

PRINCE: Cinderella, will you be mine?

CINDERELLA: Dear Prince, of course I will.

CLORINDA: Well, I knew he had no taste.

THISBE: I can't see what he sees in a walking scarecrow like her. She's not fit to be a Princess. It's ridiculous.

BUTTONS: Congratulations, Cinderella. I'm so pleased you are going to be happy at last. You deserve all the happiness in the whole wide world.

CINDERELLA: Oh, thank you Buttons, you're the best friend a girl could have.

BUTTONS: I hope you'll live happily ever after.

CINDERELLA: But you must come and live with us at the Palace.

CLORINDA:
THISBE: } Can we come too?

CINDERELLA: Can they, Prince?

PRINCE: If they promise to be good.

CLORINDA:
THISBE: } We do.

CINDERELLA: So we'll <u>all</u> live happily ever after.

PRINCE: The story's ended happily and now's the time
To bring the curtain down on Christmas pantomime.
Let's go and sing and dance and cheer and shout 'Hooray!'
For this is now fair Cinderella's Wedding Day!

THE END

CHRISTMAS PARTIES

Christmas Parties

In this book you should be able to find all the information
you need to give a successful Christmas party. Of course, all
the best parties are properly planned and prepared in advance
and to help you plan and prepare your party here are two
party timetables. Both of them are very different and both
should give you lots of fun. The timetables are for afternoon
parties, but you can give a party in the morning or the
evening just as easily. Whenever you give the party, don't be
tempted to let it go on for longer than two and a half hours.
After that long, people tend to get tired and bad-tempered!

The numbers in brackets will tell you the page where
you can find details of the particular game or trick or carol
or recipe or play. Of course, you can work out your own
party timetable, but to begin with these two may give you
some help.

Timetable 1

3.30 pm	GAMES	
	Goody Two Shoes	(page 71)
	I Spy	(page 85)
	Bag Bursting	(page 82)
4.00 pm	TEA	
	Christmas Cup	(page 46)
	Sandwiches	(page 54)
	Christmas Stars	(page 47)
	Flapjacks	(page 48)
	Frosted Fruits	(page 50)
	Chocolate Pudding	(page 44)
	Jelly	(page 49)
4.30 pm	MAGIC SHOW	
	Think of a Card	(page 60)
	Caught Cards	(page 63)
	Pound and Pencil	(page 65)
	Name the Object	(page 69)
	Magic Photo	(page 72)
	Burnt Names	(page 75)
	Magic String	(page 79)
	The Glass of Water	(page 81)
	Obedient Matchbox	(page 83)
5.00 pm	QUIZ TIME	
	Twenty Questions	(page 86)
5.20 pm	GAMES	
	Blind Man's Banquet	(page 61)
	Jingle-Jangle	(page 74)
	Merry Christmas	(page 78)
5.40 pm	THE NATIVITY PLAY	(page 92)

Timetable 2

3.30 pm   GAMES
          Blind Man's Buff   (page 73)
          Animal Snap   (page 57)
          Balloon Rockets   (page 67)

4.00 pm   TEA
          Christmas Cup   (page 46)
          Sandwiches   (page 54)
          Chocolate Crispy Cakes   (page 43)
          Marzipan Snowmen   (page 51)
          Ice Cream and Chocolate Sauce   (page 45)
          Peppermint Creams   (page 53)
          Mince Pies   (page 52)

4.30 pm   CAROL SINGING
          Away in a manger   (page 59)
          I saw three ships   (page 62)
          While shepherds watched   (page 66)
          O little town   (page 70)
          Hark! The herald angels sing   (page 80)
          O come all ye faithful   (page 84)

5.00 pm   GAMES
          Beetle   (page 58)
          Giddy Goats   (page 68)
          Old Maid   (page 76)

5.30 pm   PANTOMIME TIME
          Cinderella   (page 104)

Twenty Answers

See questions on pages 86—88

1 Prince Albert, Queen Victoria's husband.
2 Buttons.
3 Gold, frankincense and myrrh.
4 26th December, Boxing Day, is the Feast
   of Saint Stephen.
5 Widow Twankey.
6 1842.
7 6th January.
8 Two turtle-doves and three French hens.
9 On Highgate Hill.
10 King Wenceslas.
11 Rudolph, Donner, Blitzen, Dasher, Dancer, Prancer,
   Vixen, Comet, Cupid.
12 Bethlehem. Nazareth.
13 Holly and Ivy.
14 Charles Dickens. William Shakespeare.
15 *'I saw three ships come sailing in,*
   'On Christmas day, on Christmas day;
   'I saw three ships come sailing in,
   'On Christmas day in the morning'.
16 a) Friar Tuck, Little John and Will Scarlett
       are the best known
   b) The Sheriff of Nottingham.
   c) Maid Marion.
17 *'If you haven't got a penny a halfpenny will do,*
   'If you haven't got a halfpenny, God bless you!'
18 Little Jack Horner.
19 The Christmas Island that Captain Cook discovered in
   1777 is in the Pacific Ocean. There is another Christmas
   Island in the Indian Ocean.
20 MERRY CHRISTMAS AND A HAPPY NEW YEAR.

... and a happy
New Year